# The Existence

Search within

Nitinkumar Deore

BookLeaf Publishing

India | USA | UK

The Publisher and Editor shall not be liable whatsoever...

Made with ❤ on the BookLeaf Publishing Platform
www.bookleafpub.in
www.bookleafpub.com

*To my family who always supports and stands behind me.*

-NITIN

# Acknowledgement

It's a dream come true to have my poetry book published on the online platform of BookLeaf Publishing.

I'm really thankful to God, my family members and friends for supporting me.

# Preface

Sometimes in our life, we suffer a lot.
Bad situations and ups and downs in life
cause us to collapse.
But we have to keep our flow going.
My poems will make you happy and joyful.
- Nitinkumar Deore

# CONTENTS

# My soul My Mother

Hey mother!!

You left me alone
Hey mother.....
You break me whole
Hey mother .....
You were my world
You were my soul
You were my inspiration
You were my breath

But dear mother
I feel alone now
You left this world
You left me alone.....

You always told me
the story of a brave boy
who never lost his patience and joy

But mother I am not that brave boy
Please come again
To meet me
I feel lonely, Aai

Hey mother
You left me alone....
But now I've decided to act
Like that brave boy
Whose stories you told me.
I kept my mind focused and will achieve
all dreams that you've shown me.

Love you, my mother
You were, are, and will be my world always.

# If you believe you can

Feels so tough
Feels so low
Feels so uneasy
Feels so bad
Why????
Don't know but it feels like that always.

Why Does It Feel This Way?

Feels so hard, like a heavy stone,
Feels so low, as though I'm alone.
Feels so uneasy, like I can't breathe,
Feels so bad, like I've lost belief.

Why? I ask, but can't find the reason,
This weight in my heart, it feels like a season.
A storm that lingers, a shadow that stays,
Leaving me lost in countless ways.

Don't know why it feels this way,
It comes and goes, but doesn't fade away.
Yet I hold on, through pain and doubt,
Knowing one day, I'll find my way out.

Sometimes life brings these heavy days,
But within the struggle, strength always stays.
Though I don't know why it feels this way,
I'll rise again, and find my way.

But one day, I visited a temple so bright,
And read a line that ignited a light,
"If you believe, you can do anything,"
A simple truth, with power to bring.

I believed, and now I can,
Rise above, and take a stand.
The weight of doubt began to fade,
A new strength in my heart was made.

It returned my joy, energy, and fire,
Positivity burning with a deep desire.
My dreams now feel closer than before,
I believe, and that's the key to soar.

The darkness lifted, the clouds parted,
A new beginning, where hope had started.
Now, every step is filled with grace,
For I know that belief lights the way, in every
place.

No longer lost in fear or doubt,
I embrace the future, let my spirit shout.
With belief in myself, I rise once more,
I can achieve, and my dreams will soar.

# Be like Feather

When you feel heavy inside
When you feel unstable inside.....
That means
You are attacked by evil
You are attacked by ego, sorrow, and a
superiority complex.
You feel like ten heads of Ravana
like no one can kill you or nail you
As if you are a supremo

Hey, hey, friend.....
stop for a while and take a deep breath.....
You have to cleanse yourself from the
inside....
You must empty yourself from the inside
But how?
When you fill your inside world with the
light of spirituality, the darkness of evil
vanishes.

Sorrow and ego are the edges of evil
you have to conquer it with
love, sympathy, positivity and joy
Then you'd feel light as a feather.

# Mirror

If you are loving, if you are genuine,
If you are humble, if you are polite,
The world is yours, shining so bright,
A place where kindness feels just right.

But if you are rude, if you are cruel,
If you are dual, playing the fool,
The world grows distant, far away,
A cold reflection at the end of the day.

The world is like a mirror, it reflects,
As you act, it shows the effects.
If you show love, it returns to you,
A cycle of warmth, forever true.

And if you show anger, harsh and wild,
It mirrors back, like a storm beguiled.
So feel your heart full of joy and grace,
And you'll find love in every place.

With cheerfulness and a loving heart,
The world will embrace you, play its part.
You'll be lovable, kind, and true,
And the world will shine its love on you.

# The existence

A force unseen, yet deeply felt,
In every heart, where mysteries dwelt.
Beyond the stars, beyond the skies,
A superpower that never dies.

Controlling time, each fleeting hour,
Guiding life with unseen power.
In whispers soft, or nature's roar,
A presence vast, we can't ignore.

It weaves our fates, both near and far,
Our hopes and dreams, each tiny scar.
In love, in loss, in every breath,
A silent guide through life and death.

Call it God, or fate, or chance,
An endless, boundless cosmic dance.
The existence flows through all we see,
The source of life's great mystery.

# Clean Heart

Clean your heart, free from dirt,
Let go of anger, heal the hurt.
Wash away the pain and fear,
Embrace the love that's always near.

Let kindness bloom, let hatred fade,
A peaceful soul is gently made.
Release the chains of envy and greed,
Plant the seeds of every good deed.

Forgive the past, let grudges go,
In purity, let your spirit glow.
A heart that's clean, so light and free,
Holds the key to true harmony.

The world will shine, as bright as dawn,
When hearts unburdened carry on.
So cleanse your heart, make a new start,
For joy and love will soon impart.

# Cage

When you scream, you lose your dreams,
Torn apart by anger's streams.
The fire within, though fierce it burns,
Leaves only ashes, no returns.

The voice that rises, sharp and loud,
Drowns the whispers of the proud.
A heart once calm, now lost in rage,
A soul confined within its cage.

But silence holds a healing grace,
A chance to mend, a steady pace.
For when you pause, and gently breathe,
You find the strength to calmly lead.

So hold your tongue, let peace begin,
A tranquil mind, a world within.
For dreams are lost in fury's gleam,
But found in love's enduring stream.

# Live like a monk

Live like a monk, serene and still,
Master your heart, bend it to will.
Let negativity go, let it flee,
Embrace the light of harmony.

Detach from greed, let go of hate,
Walk the path where peace awaits.
In silence, find the strength to grow,
Like a river's calm and steady flow.

Seek no more than inner peace,
Let worldly desires slowly cease.
With a heart that's pure and mind so clear,
You'll find true joy, far and near.

Like a monk, let simplicity reign,
Find your peace amidst the pain.
For in the quiet, you'll always know,
True contentment, in its gentle glow.

# Always be positive

Don't think negative, always be positive,
Life is a gift, so bright and so vivid.
Each day a chance, a brand-new start,
A canvas to paint with a hopeful heart.

The sun will rise, no matter the night,
Filling the world with endless light.
In every trial, there's wisdom to gain,
Through every storm, comes sunshine again.

So embrace the journey, come what may,
With a heart full of hope, lead the way.
For life's true beauty is found inside,
In the positive thoughts, you choose to guide.

When challenges arise, stand tall and strong,
For with positivity, you can't go wrong.
Believe in yourself, trust in your power,
And watch your dreams bloom, hour by hour.

# My Friends

Friends are the treasure,
Give always pleasure.
They are not relatives,
But solve every issue with their initiatives.

In joy and sorrow, they're always near,
Their words of comfort wipe every tear.
Through thick and thin, they choose to stay,
Guiding us gently along the way.

A bond unspoken, yet deeply true,
Friends are the blessings life gives you.
With every laugh and every shared pain,
True friendship is a constant gain.

They lift you up when you fall,
Answer your heart's every call.
So cherish your friends, near or far,
For they are the brightest of every star.

# Family

Family is the pillar,
Always there, a soothing healer.
Through every storm, they stand by your side,
A source of strength, a constant guide.

Their love is pure, their care runs deep,
A bond eternal, forever to keep.
In laughter, in tears, in joy, in pain,
Family's support will always remain.

With open arms and hearts so wide,
Family is life's greatest pride.
Through all of life's highs and lows,
Their love is the light that forever glows.

In every moment, in every stride,
Family's the anchor, always beside.
No matter the road, the journey, the fight,
They'll be the beacon, shining bright.

# When I feel afraid

When I feel afraid
I call upon the Almighty
I talk with him and focus
On him
He is the powerhouse of
Peace and patience
He told me
Don't be afraid
Always keep mum and
Start your way
Don't be afraid
Just speak with me and
Start your day
I am within you
And always behind you
So keep going on and on.

# Support system

You are my strength, my guiding light,
In every moment, day and night.
Through every trial, you stand by me,
A pillar of love, so strong, so free.

You are my support system, firm and true,
In every challenge, I turn to you.
With your love, I find my way,
You lift me up, and brighten my day.

Oh dear, you're my heart's embrace,
In your presence, I find my place.
Your faith in me gives me wings to fly,
With you by my side, I touch the sky.

Through every storm, you're my calm,
Your love, a healing, soothing balm.
I am strong, because you believe,
With you, there's nothing I can't achieve.

# Cloudy storm

When clouds surround,
And darkness stays,
Hold on with patience,
Through shadowed days.

The blackest night
Will pass in time,
The sun will rise,
And the skies will shine.

Through winds that howl
And tempests strong,
Your heart will learn
Where you belong.

For every storm
Has its own end,
And every tear
The light will mend.

So face the clouds,
Don't let them stay
The sun will guide
Your steps each day.

# Prayers

I swear, prayers are fine,
They will reach you at cloud nine.
Hope is the best remedy,
It creates endless possibility.

When shadows fall and doubts arise,
Lift your gaze to brighter skies.
Each whispered plea, each silent word,
In realms unseen, they're always heard.

The storms may rage, the winds may cry,
Yet hope will soar, it cannot die.
It mends the heart, it soothes the soul,
It makes the broken spirit whole.

Faith will guide you, step by step,
Through trials deep where tears are kept.
Prayers will light the darkest way,
And bring you to a brighter day.

So hold on tight, through thick and thin,
The battle fought is one you'll win.
For prayers and hope, like stars above,
Will lead you to a life of love.

# Let it flow

Finally, I come to the conclusion,
That life has its own flow.
Do not get stuck on anything;
Let the flow softly grow.

The rivers run, the winds will change,
The tides will rise and fall.
Resisting only brings us pain,
But trust can heal it all.

Each moment holds a lesson clear,
Each turn a path unknown.
Surrender to the rhythm here,
And you'll find you've truly grown.

So let life lead, its currents guide,
Through valleys deep and high.
For in its flow, the heart resides,
Beneath the endless sky.

# Trust

The rivers twist, the winds may sway,
Yet all returns in time.
Each fleeting moment shapes the way,
Each loss will birth a rhyme.

The branches bend, the stars will fade,
And storms may come and pass.
But still, the roots remain unshaken,
Anchored deep beneath the grass.

We hold too tight to fleeting things,
Afraid to let them part.
But life's true beauty softly sings
In the freeing of the heart.

So let life lead, like oceans wide,
Unfolding as it will.
Resist the urge to fight the tide,
And find your purpose still.

For peace is found not in control,
But in trusting the unknown.
Life flows as one, a moving whole,
And we are never alone.

# Ego

Ego is the barrier,
A shadow in disguise.
It blinds the heart, it clouds the mind,
And fuels deceitful lies.


It builds a wall around the soul,
A fortress made of pride.
Yet inside lies a hollow void,
Where fears and doubts reside.

Ego destroys what love creates,
It burns the bridges near.
It turns a friend into a foe,
And stirs the seeds of fear.

So break the chains, let ego fall,
Its weight is far too great.
Embrace the strength of humbleness,
Before it is too late.

For life rewards the tender heart,
The one who learns to bow.
To grow, to heal, to truly start,
Let grace and peace endow.

# Don't give up

The days will definitely come,
When all your struggles are overcome.
The hard work you've put, the pain you've known,
Will bloom into rewards you've always been shown.

Through every setback, every fall,
Know that your time will come, after all.
The road may be steep, the night may be long,
But with every step, you grow more strong.

Keep your spirit high, your heart full of hope,
For success is a ladder, and you're learning to cope.
Your dreams will come true, you'll rise above,
For the future is shaped by the power of love.

So don't give up, keep pushing through,
Your days will come, and they'll be true.
With every challenge, you'll find your way,
And the dawn of success will light your day.

# Keep place back

I always keep my place back,
Humble and steady, I stay on track.
I always strive to be a gentleman,
Living with grace, as best I can.


I keep myself grounded, stay low and true,
Feeling peace in all I do.
For I know the Almighty walks by my side,
With Him, I have nothing to hide.


He always does what's best for me,
Even when life feels like a stormy sea.
When sadness knocks and troubles rise,
He whispers strength, through silent skies.

"Don't put down your weapons," He says,
"Do your duty through every phase.
Depend on Me, and trust My plan,
I'll lift you higher than you ever can."


And with His words, I feel complete,
Even in struggles, I find my feet.
So friends, always do your duty with pride,
Let faith in Him be your guide.


For the Almighty's love is vast and true,
He will always do the best for you.
Stay faithful, humble, and strong each day,
And He will light your every way.

# Rat race

This is a big rush
This is the big fight
This is the big competition
This is the rat race tight
Hey friend, stop—
Be calm and cool
Just need to think
Why you are doing this
Why are you running
Behind money
Power and property?
What will it give you?
It gives nothing but more desires
It gives nothing but more lust
And brings dissatisfaction and thrust.
So friend, feel free....
Feel happy.....
Do your job silently.

Take time for health
Physically and mentally
Love your family and friends
Feel comfortably
Be satisfied, always.

# Respect

Give respect, take respect,
This is the rule we must reflect.
In every word, in every deed,
Respect is the foundation of every need.


When you honor others, you honor yourself,
It brings peace and joy, like a quiet wealth.
The more you give, the more you receive,
In a world of respect, all hearts believe.


Treat others kindly, with patience and care,
And you'll find that respect is always there.
For this simple truth, we all must see,
Give respect, and respect will come to you.


Respect the young, the old, the wise,
See the world through open eyes.
In giving respect, we build a bond,
A connection that lasts, deep and strong.

When you give, it comes back to you,
Like sunlight breaking through the blue.
A heart that gives will never lack,
For respect always finds its way back.


So let's make respect our guiding star,
In our actions, near and far.
For in this world, one truth we know:
Give respect, and watch it grow.

# Life

Life is a river, winding and wide,
A journey we take, with the current as a
guide.
Through valleys of joy, and mountains of
strife,
Each bend is a chapter, the story of life.


It whispers at dawn, as the sun starts to rise,
A canvas of hope beneath endless skies.
It roars in the storm, when the shadows
prevail,
Yet strength lies in rowing, through the
fiercest gale.


Life is a garden, where dreams start to bloom,
In the soil of effort, dispelling the gloom.
Each failure a lesson, each tear a seed,
That nurtures the courage to flourish and
lead.

It's laughter at dusk, with stars shining bright,
A dance in the dark, a spark in the night.
Life is a mosaic, of moments combined,
A masterpiece crafted, by heart and by mind.


So cherish the seasons, fleeting and grand,
For life is a treasure, a gift in your hand.
Embrace every heartbeat, the highs and the
lows,
In the rhythm of living, true beauty grows.

# Purpose

What is the purpose, the reason, the goal,
That breathes into being and kindles the soul?
Is it wealth, is it power, or fleeting acclaim,
Or something more subtle, beyond worldly
fame?

To live is to learn, to grow and to give,
To find in each moment a reason to live.
To love without bounds, to seek and to share,
To lift one another, to show that we care.

It's the spark of creation, the quest for the
true,
The joy in the journey, in all that we do.
It's the courage to dream, to rise and to fall,
To hear life's faint whispers, and answer its
call.

The purpose is kindness, the purpose is grace,
To leave gentle footprints in time's endless
space.

To kindle the fire that brightens the night,
To weave through the shadows and bring
forth the light.

So seek not in riches, in fame, or in pride,
But look in your heart, let it be your guide.
The purpose of life, in its infinite art,
Is written in love, in the depths of your heart.

# Why we take birth

Why We Take Birth on Earth: A Poem

Why do we come to this world so wide,
A fleeting moment in time's endless tide?
Is it chance, is it fate, or a grander design,
A purpose unseen, a thread divine?

We take birth to learn, to grow and explore,
To open new windows, to unlock each door.
To feel the warmth of the sun's golden rays,
And dance in the rain on life's fleeting days.

We are here to love, to give and to care,
To build bridges of hope, and burdens to
share.
To marvel at stars in the vast, endless sky,
And wonder the meaning of where and why.

We're born to create, to dream and aspire,
To kindle the world with our inner fire.
To leave it brighter and kinder than we came,
A legacy etched in the whispers of our name.


We take birth on Earth, a school for the soul,
To seek out our truth, to be part of the whole.
Each life is a chapter, each moment a part,
Of the infinite story written in the heart.


So cherish this journey, this chance, this grace,
To walk on this earth, to embrace this space.
For every birth is a gift, a new chance to be,
A note in the song of eternity.

# Love

Love is the only remedy,
To build up your relationships endlessly.
It's the bond that heals all scars,
A light that shines, no matter how far.


Through every trial, love remains,
It breaks the barriers, eases the pains.
In laughter and in tears, it grows,
A river of warmth, wherever it flows.


Love is patience, love is trust,
In it, all wounds turn to dust.
It's the foundation, strong and true,
That holds two hearts and makes them new.

So nurture it with care each day,
Let it guide you, come what may.
For love is the key, the only way,
To make relationships forever stay.

# Become the sea

Let us become the sea, my friend,
A boundless stretch with no clear end.
Where sky meets water, dreams arise,
And waves reflect the open skies.


Let us dissolve in the ocean's call,
No edges, no borders to mark us at all.
The salt of sorrow, the spray of glee,
All merge as one in the endless sea.


We'll hold the ships, we'll cradle the moon,
Dance to the tides, hum ancient tunes.
Each wave a heartbeat, each swell a song,
A rhythm eternal, deep and strong.

No need for words, no need for land,
Just the shifting sands and the meeting
strand.
Come, my friend, let's drift and be—
The infinite soul of the eternal sea.

# Noise within you

The noise resides within you,
Today, cast it out.
The chains that bind you to yourself,
Today, break them open wide.


Dare to cross your boundaries,
Have the courage to move beyond.
The fire hidden within you,
Unleash it upon the world.


Leave behind fear and doubt,
Witness the flight of your aspirations.
Your resolve is with you,
Just focus on your determination.

Turn the noise into silence,
And then behold the miracle.
The echo of your hard work,
Will shake the entire world.

# Keep calm

I keep calm, but do not mistake,
This silence holds the strength I make.
In storms of chaos, I stand tall,
With quiet resolve, I face it all.


Not every battle needs a shout,
Not every fear is worth a doubt.
My calm is not a sign of fear,
It shows my will to persevere.


The fire inside burns steady, bright,
Patience is my shield, my might.
I choose to think before I fight,
To act with wisdom, not with spite.


A storm within, I hold it tight,
A roaring sea, yet still as night.

# I will do my best

I will do my best, come what may,
No fear or doubt will block my way.
With every step, I'll rise and fight,
Chasing dreams with all my might.


I will never hesitate or fall,
Through every challenge, I'll stand tall.
With courage strong and heart so true,
I'll pave my path, I'll see it through.


The storms may roar, the winds may sway,
But I'll keep moving, day by day.
For in my soul, a fire will burn,
With every lesson, I'll learn and turn.


I promise myself, I'll never break,
For every stride is mine to take.
I will do my best, I'll give my all,
Until I reach my final call.

# Excellence

Keep your eye on excellence, steady and clear,
Let purpose guide you, let go of fear.
With focus sharp and heart so true,
The best version of yourself will shine
through.


Rise above the noise, the doubt, the delay,
Step by step, carve your way.
Success is near, just stay in the race,
And soon you'll find your destined place.


For those who strive, who dare to dream,
Life becomes more than it may seem.
Keep your eye on excellence, let it be,
Your path to greatness, your destiny.

# Human being

You are a human, born to think,
To rise above, not merely sink.
With mind and heart, a gift so rare,
To show the world you truly care.


Don't live in anger, greed, or spite,
Choose what's just, choose what's right.
For instincts wild are not your chain,
You hold the power to ease the pain.


An animal acts without a thought,
But you've been blessed with lessons taught.
Compassion, wisdom—let them reign,
Don't let your actions go in vain.


So walk the path that leads to light,
Be the hope, and shine so bright.
You're a human, born to lead,
Sow the love and not the greed.

# Are you from a rural background?

"Are you from a rural background?" they ask,
Their eyes a mirror, a silent mask.
As if the roots that shaped my way,
Are less than theirs in some grand play.


Yes, I am from fields wide and free,
Where winds whisper tales to every tree.
Where stars at night outshine the glare,
Of urban lights and city's care.


I know the soil, its earthy scent,
The honest toil, the life well spent.
My hands may show the work they've done,
But my heart reflects the rising sun.

Your gaze may hold a quiet doubt,
But I hold pride, without a shout.
For rural veins run deep and strong,
A heritage that sings its song.


So ask again, and I'll reply,
With grounded feet and a head held high.
Yes, I am from a rural land,
Rich in spirit, bold in stand.

# Crowd

In the crowd, where voices collide,
Focus on yourself, let your wisdom guide.
Amid the noise, find your own sound,
Grow with purpose, steady and profound.


Don't compare your path to another's way,
The sun and moon both shine in their sway.
Water your dreams with patience and care,
For growth is quiet, yet beyond compare.


Learn from the storm, embrace the rain,
Every fall is a step toward gain.
Care for others, but don't forget,
To nurture the soul where your hopes are set.


In the crowd, stay calm, stay true,
Your light will shine, and guide you through.
Growth and care, a delicate art,
Begin with focus and an open heart.

# My love, my wife

Hey my love, my dearest wife,
You are the joy that lights my life.
In every breath, in all I do,
I always care, my love is true.


Through highs and lows, I'll stand by you,
With every storm, we'll see it through.
My heart beats only to adore,
With every day, I love you more.


Your smile, your touch, your gentle way,
Brighten my world, night or day.
You are my strength, my guiding star,
No matter the distance, near or far.


My love is pure, it knows no end,
A promise eternal, my soulmate, my friend.
Hey my love, my cherished wife,
You are my forever, my whole life.

# Hey my daughter

Hey my daughter, my precious part,
You are my soul, you are my heart.
With your laughter, my world does mend,
You are my pure, innocent friend.

Your tiny hands hold all my dreams,
Your sparkling eyes are love's true beams.
In your smile, I find my peace,
In your embrace, all worries cease.

You teach me to find joy in simple things,
The magic of life that childhood brings.
Hey my daughter, my shining light,
With you, my days are warm and bright.

I'll guide your steps, but let you fly,
Chasing dreams across the sky.
Forever my love, my heart will send,
To you, my daughter, my innocent friend.

# My son

Hey my son, my precious gem,
You shine brighter than any diadem.
I always care, with love so true,
Every heartbeat, I pray for you.


Your dreams are stars, I see them soar,
I'll cheer for you forevermore.
Through every step, in all you do,
My love will always follow you.


You are my strength, my greatest pride,
A bond unbreakable, side by side.
Hey my son, my life's bright flame,
Forever and always, you are my gem.


Through every step, I'll hold your hand,
Guide your way, help you stand.
Your dreams are precious, your path is wide,
In your success, I swell with pride.

You are my joy, my priceless gem,
A crown of love, my brightest emblem.
Hey my son, remember this true,
No one will ever love you like I do.

# Selflessness

Selflessness is best for society's soul,
A noble path, a virtuous goal.
When hearts unite to give and share,
Prosperity blooms, beyond compare.


The hands that serve, the hearts that care,
Create a world that's just and fair.
With kindness sown in every deed,
We meet each other's deepest need.


Selfless acts, though quiet, grow,
A brighter future begins to show.
For in the giving, love takes root,
And society reaps its sweetest fruit.

So let us strive, with unity,
To build a world of harmony.
Selflessness is best, this truth we see,
For it develops lasting prosperity.

# The price of success

If you want success, there's a price to pay,
Through effort and toil, day by day.
Dreams aren't built on wishes alone,
They're carved with sweat, your will, your own.


Hard work is the currency, the only way,
To turn the night into a brighter day.
Each step you climb, each hurdle you face,
Brings you closer to your destined place.


No shortcuts exist, no easy lane,
It's persistence that conquers pain.
So rise each morning with fire inside,
And let your dedication be your guide.

Success demands the best you can give,
Through hard work, you truly live.
For when you've paid the price it takes,
You'll hold the success no storm can shake.

# Walk on the path of Dharma

Always walk on the path of Dharma, stay true,
This is the wisdom Krishna gives you.
In the Bhagavad Gita, He makes it clear,
Righteous actions will bring no fear.

If you walk on Dharma's sacred way,
Your karma will shine, pure as day.
With honesty, kindness, and a heart so strong,
You'll find peace where you belong.

Dharma guides, no matter how tough,
Through storms of life, it's more than enough.
With every step, let virtue lead,
Planting the world with every good deed.

Krishna's words, a timeless lore,
Remind us all of what we're here for.
Follow the Dharma, and you will see,
A life of purpose, pure and free.

# My duty, My Nation

For me, my duty will always come first,
A sacred fire, an unending thirst.
To serve with honor, to stand and fight,
For my nation's glory, my guiding light.


My nation first, above all I hold dear,
Its pride and safety, my greatest cheer.
Through storms and trials, I'll stand tall,
To protect its honor, I'll give my all.


No sacrifice too big, no effort too small,
When my country calls, I give it my all.
For in its freedom, my soul does rest,
My duty first, my nation is blessed.

Let the world see, let the future say,
I lived for my country, come what may.
For me, my duty and nation align,
A bond eternal, forever divine.

# Life, an amazing gift

Life is an amazing gift, so rare,
A treasure beyond compare.
Precious, valuable, a chance to grow,
A journey where wonders constantly flow.


Keep your mindset steady and strong,
Through trials and triumphs, carry along.
For every challenge, a lesson to learn,
In every setback, a chance to turn.


Cherish the moments, big and small,
Live with gratitude, embrace it all.
With courage in heart and dreams in sight,
Life will shine with endless light.


Remember, this gift is yours to embrace,
A journey of love, hope, and grace.
Life is amazing, let it unfold,
A story of strength, brave and bold.

# Keep your heart full of faith

Keep your heart full of faith.
It will guide and uplift you.
Through darkest nights and toughest days,
Faith will light your path and ways.


Faith gives you joy, a peaceful mind,
A treasure within, so rare to find.
It heals the soul, it calms the storm,
Keeps your spirit alive and warm.


When doubts arise, and hope feels small,
Faith will catch you, never let you fall.
With trust in life, and love as your guide,
Happiness and strength will walk beside.

So keep your heart steadfast and bright,
With faith, you'll conquer every fight.
It gives you courage, a reason to strive,
A heart full of faith keeps dreams alive.

# Smile

A smile is a gift so pure and true,
It wipes away the darkest blue.
A simple curve, yet full of might,
It spreads hope and endless light.


It wipes the tears, it heals the pain,
It brings the sun after the rain.
In every heart, it plants a seed,
Of love, of joy, of every good deed.


A smile costs nothing, yet gives so much,
A tender glance, a gentle touch.
So wear it proudly, let it show,
And watch how kindness starts to grow.

Smile is the best, a treasure divine,
A language of hearts, yours and mine.
It wipes the sorrow, the fear, the fight,
And fills the world with pure delight.

# College days

Golden days of college life,
Are filled with joy and free from strife.
Friendships bloom, and dreams take flight,
In halls of learning, hearts ignite.


Endless laughter, and carefree talks,
Midnight walks, boards and chalks.
Chasing knowledge, and moments grand,
Together we stand, hand in hand.


The lectures, the tests, the late-night grind,
All weave memories in your mind.
The struggles, the fun, the moments bright,
Are treasures you'll cherish with all your
might.

The golden days are fleeting, true,
But their essence stays, forever new.
They shape who we are, and what we'll
become,
The golden days of college—where our
journey begun.


So let's embrace them, with hearts full of
grace,
For in those days, we found our place.
Golden memories, forever they stay,
The best of times, in every way.

# Our INDIA

Let's unite, let's stand strong,
Together we'll right every wrong.
Hand in hand, with hearts as one,
Our journey to greatness has begun.


Our India will rise, proud and free,
A beacon of hope for the world to see.
With unity's power, we'll break every chain,
Through trials and storms, through joy and
pain.


Let's build a nation with love and light,
Where every soul can shine very bright.
With courage, wisdom, and resolve so tall,
Our India will prosper and inspire all.

Let's unite, let's stand as a team,
Turning every dream into a gleam.
For our India, we'll give our best,
Together, we'll rise above the rest.


India, India, a word that inspires every soul
Let's fill up the gaps, make hearts whole
Keep your head high and don't be shy
Indian TIRANGA will always fly high!

# The value of Honesty

Most of the time, we think it's true,
That honesty holds no value.
But friend, let me tell you straight,
Honesty shapes a heart so great.


The world may seem to ignore the kind,
But truth and virtue always shine.
An honest person, steady and strong,
Will find their place where they belong.


For trust is built on truth alone,
Where honest seeds are always sown.
The path may be hard, the climb may be
steep,
But integrity's treasure is yours to keep.

So never doubt the value you bring,
When honesty is your guiding string.
Friend, the world needs hearts like yours,
To open the light through honest doors.

# Be free and Frank

Lastly, I want to tell you, my friend,
Be free and frank, let nothing pretend.
Speak your truth, let your heart be clear,
For honesty and openness, there's no fear.


Don't keep anything locked inside,
Let your thoughts and feelings collide.
A mind at peace, with nothing to hide,
Is the truest way to stand with pride.


Be free in spirit, bold and strong,
Don't let silence be where you belong.
Speak your heart, let your voice rise,
And live with no regrets, no disguise.

So be free, be frank, and walk with grace,
With an open heart, you'll find your place.
Release the weight, let your mind unwind,
For peace and joy you will surely find.

# What is success?

What is success?
It is not about getting power or fame,
Not wealth, title, or a fleeting claim.
Success is not the things we own,
But the peace and joy we've truly grown.


It's in the work, the effort, the strive,
The dreams we chase, that make us feel alive.
It's in the moments we rise above,
And the kindness shared, from heart to heart.


Success is found in how we live,
In what we give, and what we forgive.
It's the love we nurture, the bonds we create,
The lives we touch, the paths we navigate.

It's not about the title, or the gold,
But the strength and wisdom we unfold.
Success is a journey, not a destination,
It's the heart's true measure, in every
situation.

www.ingramcontent.com/pod-product-compliance
Lightning Source LLC
La Vergne TN
LVHW010018200726
843495LV00015B/1828